W9-BBC-389

Middle Eastern Migration

Deborah Kent

Raintree

Chicago, Illinois

www.heinemannraintree.com
Visit our website to find out
more information about
Heinemann-Raintree books.

To order:
☎ Phone 888-454-2279
💻 Visit www.heinemannraintree.com
to browse our catalog and order online.

© 2012 Raintree
an imprint of Capstone Global Library, LLC
Chicago, Illinois

All rights reserved. No part of this publication may be
reproduced or transmitted in any form or by any means,
electronic or mechanical, including photocopying, recording,
taping, or any information storage and retrieval system,
without permission in writing from the publisher.

Edited by Louise Galpine, Abby Colich, and Diyan Leake
Designed by Richard Parker
Original illustrations © Capstone Global Library Ltd 2011
Illustrated by Jeff Edwards
Picture research by Mica Brancic

Originated by Capstone Global Library Ltd
Printed and bound in China by CTPS

15 14 13 12 11
10 9 8 7 6 5 4 3 2

Library of Congress Cataloging-in-Publication Data
Kent, Deborah.
  Middle Eastern migration / Deborah Kent.
    p. cm.—(Children's true stories: migration)
  Includes bibliographical references and index.
  ISBN 978-1-4109-4073-5 (hc)—ISBN 978-1-4109-4079-7 (pb)
  1. Refugee children—Middle East—Case studies—Juvenile
literature. 2. Middle East—Emigration and immigration—Case
studies—Juvenile literature. I. Title.
  JV8739.K46 2012
  305.23086'9140956—dc22   2010039323

Acknowledgments
We would like to thank the following for permission to
reproduce photographs: Corbis p. 9 (© Bettmann); Getty
Images pp. 6 (Time Life Pictures/Dmitri Kessel), 12 (AFP
Photo/Joseph Eid), 14 (AFP Photo/Nabil Ismail), 15 (AFP
Photo/Joseph Barrak), 16 (AFP Photo/Marai Shah), 17 (AFP
Photo/Marai Shah), 18 (Paula Bronstein), 21 (The Christian
Science Monitor/John Nordell), 22 (Mario Tama), 24 (Chris
Hondros), 26 (AFP Photo/Mahmoud Zayat), 27 (AFP Photo/
Nicola Touahmeh); Dalia Landau p. 11; Reuters pp. 8 (© STR
New), 10 (© David Silverman), 19 (Erik de Castro); Athraa
Yalda p. 25.

Cover photograph of Palestinians riding in a vehicle with their
belongings as they leave their house in Rafah, in the southern
Gaza Strip, January 12, 2009, reproduced with permission of
Reuters (Ibraheem Abu Mustafa).

We would like to acknowledge the following sources of
material: pp. 6–11 from *The Lemon Tree: An Arab, a Jew,
and the Heart of the Middle East* by Sandy Tolan (New York:
Bloomsbury, 2002); pp. 12–15 from *Human Cargo: A Journey
Among Refugees* by Caroline Morehead (New York: Picador/
Henry Holt, 2005); pp. 16–20 from *The Story of My Life: An
Afghan Girl on the Other Side of the Sky* by Farah Ahmedi with
Tamim Ansary (New York: Simon Spotlight Entertainment,
2005); pp. 22–25 from an email exchange with Athraa Naeil
Yalda, June 1–12, 2010.

We would like to thank Professor Sarah Chinn for her
invaluable help in the preparation of this book.

Every effort has been made to contact copyright holders
of material reproduced in this book. Any omissions will
be rectified in subsequent printings if notice is given to
the publisher.

Disclaimer
All the Internet addresses (URLs) given in this book were valid
at the time of going to press. However, due to the dynamic
nature of the Internet, some addresses may have changed, or
sites may have changed or ceased to exist since publication.
While the author and publisher regret any inconvenience this
may cause readers, no responsibility for any such changes can
be accepted by either the author or the publisher.

Contents

DAILY LIFE

Read here to learn what life was like for the children in these stories, and the impact that migrating had at home and at school.

NUMBER CRUNCHING

Find out the details about migration and the numbers of people involved.

Migrants' Lives

Read these boxes to find out what happened to the children in this book when they grew up.

HELPING HAND

Find out how people and organizations have helped children to migrate.

On the Scene

Read eyewitness accounts of migration in the migrants' own words.

Some words are printed in bold, **like this**. You can find out what they mean by looking in the glossary on page 30.

Finding a Safe Place

War is a terrible tragedy. It brings injury and death to countless men and women who serve as soldiers. It also hurts **civilians** (people who are not in the armed forces). War causes millions of civilians to become **refugees**. A refugee is someone who is forced to leave home to find safety, often outside his or her country.

The Middle East

The region known as the Middle East is home to three of the world's great religions: **Judaism**, **Christianity**, and **Islam**. It is a beautiful region where farmers grow olive and lemon trees. Yet the Middle East has been the scene of cruel warfare for many years.

Wars in the Middle East have led to five million people leaving their homes. These people, often families with children, have been forced to leave their homes, friends, and possessions behind. Some live in tents or hastily built houses in neighboring countries. Some find new homes in faraway lands such as Canada, the United Kingdom, and the United States.

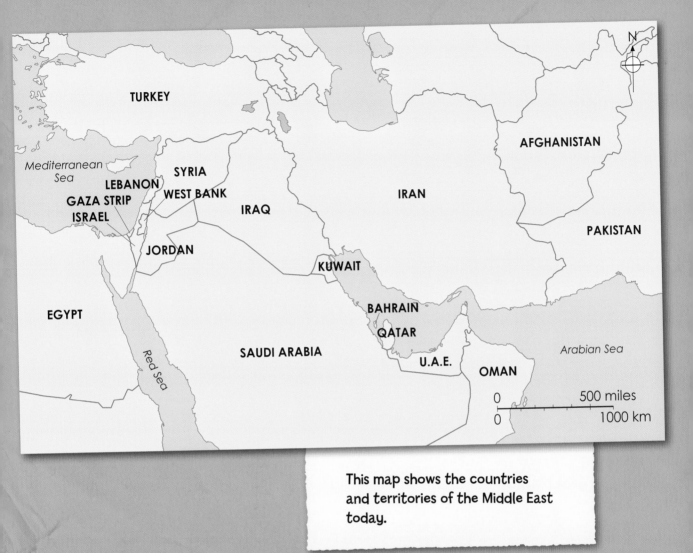

This map shows the countries and territories of the Middle East today.

NUMBER CRUNCHING

The Middle East extends for some 8,000 kilometers (5,000 miles) from west to east and some 3,200 kilometers (2,000 miles) from north to south.

Palestine: 1948

Bashir Khairi and his family were **Muslims**. They lived in the city of Al-Ramla, in Palestine.

While Bashir was a baby, **World War II** raged in Europe. More than six million Jews were murdered under the German **dictator** Adolf Hitler. The Jews who survived wanted a homeland where they and their children would be safe.

This is a view of the port of Haifa in the years before the 1948 Israeli-Palestinian War.

When the war ended, many countries formed an organization called the **United Nations (UN)**. In 1948 the UN gave part of Palestine to the Jews as the new state of Israel.

Fleeing to safety

War soon broke out between Israel and Palestine. Bashir's family was forced to flee from their home in Al-Ramla. Young Bashir was sure that soon they would all return.

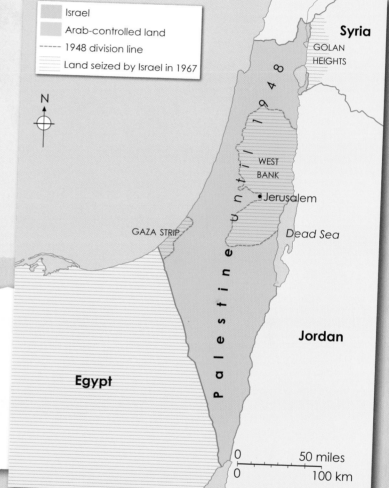

Israel
Arab-controlled land
1948 division line
Land seized by Israel in 1967

Syria
GOLAN HEIGHTS

N

Palestine until 1948

WEST BANK

•Jerusalem

GAZA STRIP

Dead Sea

Egypt

Jordan

0   50 miles
0   100 km

This map shows how the UN divided Palestine into two states in 1948. It also shows the land that Israel seized in 1967.

HELPING HAND

Like most children in Al-Ramla, Bashir had many relatives who lived nearby. When the Khairi family became refugees, it was hard for all the relatives to stay together. Bashir's parents did everything they could to help the family survive.

An unsettled life

Bashir and his family joined around 200,000 other refugees in the Palestinian city of Ramallah. The Khairis lived in a small rented room. Thousands of other families were not even that lucky. They slept in barns, in caves, or alongside roads.

Carrying their belongings, Palestinians flee from their village after the outbreak of the Israeli-Palestinian War.

After several months, Bashir and his family joined thousands more refugees in Gaza City. Bashir's father made furniture for refugee families. His mother and sisters sewed clothes to sell. Women in the family had never worked outside the home before.

Longing for home

Bashir and his sisters went to school in a tent. They sat on the dirt floor and listened to the teacher. Each morning they recited a poem about their homeland:

Our aim is to return,
Death does not frighten us,
Palestine is ours,
We shall never forget her.

This is a Palestinian refugee camp in Amman, Jordan, in 1948.

HELPING HAND

Many countries sent food for the Palestinian refugees. **Volunteers** in Europe and the United States sent tents, medicine, and other supplies. The UN Relief and Works Agency continues to help Palestinian refugees to this day.

A house and a dream

Bashir Khairi lived in Gaza City and later went back to Ramallah. He never gave up the hope of returning to live in Al-Ramla.

When he was 25 years old, Bashir visited the house in Al-Ramla where he was born. He met the Israeli family who now lived there. In the courtyard he picked a lemon from a tree that his father planted long ago. Bashir and the family's daughter, Dalia, became friends. They wrote letters to each other for many years.

This is a Palestinian throwing stones at Israeli troops on the anniversary of the 1987 uprising called the War of Stones.

Bashir Khairi

Bashir Khairi became a lawyer in Ramallah. He helped organizations that sought to regain Palestinian land. Some of these organizations used violence to fight Israel. Bashir was arrested and spent years in prison.

Later, Bashir and his friend Dalia turned the house in Al-Ramla into a daycare center for Muslim children. They hoped that the house would become a place where Palestinians and Israelis could meet and get to know each other.

These people are at the summer camp run at Bashir's childhood home in Al-Ramla.

11

Lebanon: 1960

Tariq Halimi grew up in a tent in Shatila, a refugee camp in southern Lebanon. Most of the families in the camp were refugees from Palestine. They had been forced to leave their homes during the 1948 war between Palestine and Israel.

Palestinian refugees live in poverty in the Shatila Refugee Camp near Beirut, Lebanon. The camp has been there so long that it has almost become a town.

Life in Shatila

Sometimes Tariq helped his father flatten empty oil drums. They used the metal to make walls, doors, and roofs. Little by little they turned their tent into a shack that could give them more shelter.

Like most children in Shatila, Tariq wore clothes made from old flour sacks. His mother decorated his shirts with the Palestinian flag. She wanted him to be proud of his homeland.

Memories of another time

Every day Tariq listened to his parents talk about Balad Al-Sheik, the beautiful village where they once lived. He had never seen Balad Al-Sheik, but he felt as though he knew every house and street.

NUMBER CRUNCHING

In 2010 the United Nations Relief and Works Agency said that there were 4,766,670 Palestinian refugees. These refugees were mainly people or families who lost their homes in the 1948 Israeli–Palestinian War and their descendants.

A rebel organization

When Tariq was 14, he and his friends formed a soccer team. **Fatah** was a group of Palestinian **rebels**. They wanted to overthrow Israel by using violence. They got teenage soccer players to join them. Tariq became active with the Fatah group. He learned to fight and dreamed of regaining lost Palestinian land.

Children play soccer in the ruins of Shatila Refugee Camp after the Israeli attack of 1982.

When Tariq Halimi was 18 years old, he enrolled at the American University in Beirut, Lebanon. He later left his studies to work with Palestinian political organizations.

The people of Israel had worked hard to build their new country. They remembered the murders of millions of Jewish men, women, and children in Europe during World War II. They vowed that such a thing must never happen again.

War in Lebanon

When Israel learned that Palestinian rebels were living in Lebanon, Israeli troops invaded Lebanon in 1982. Thousands of Palestinians and Lebanese died in the fighting. Tariq escaped to the United Kingdom. He was a refugee again.

Students enjoy life on the peaceful campus of the American University in Beirut.

Tariq Halimi

Tariq Halimi became a successful printer in Oxford, England. He still thinks of himself as Palestinian, but he knows that he will never live in the land his parents loved so much.

Afghanistan: 2002

When Farah Ahmedi was growing up in Afghanistan, her country was torn apart by war. Rebel groups fought among themselves for control of the land and resources.

A terrible injury

Farah lived with her family in a compound (area with a wall around it) in Kabul, Afghanistan's capital. One day when she was seven years old, she took a shortcut to school. She stepped on a **landmine** and it exploded. Her leg was badly injured. Doctors had to remove her injured leg and give her an **artificial** one.

Fleeing the Taliban

The fighting in Afghanistan grew worse and worse. A group called the **Taliban** came to power. The Taliban would not let girls go to school, and they punished many people. Life became very difficult. Farah's father and sisters were killed when their house was bombed. Finally, Farah and her mother fled over the border into Pakistan, where they lived in a refugee camp.

Women walk in the Old City section of Kabul, covered from head to toe, as ordered by the Taliban.

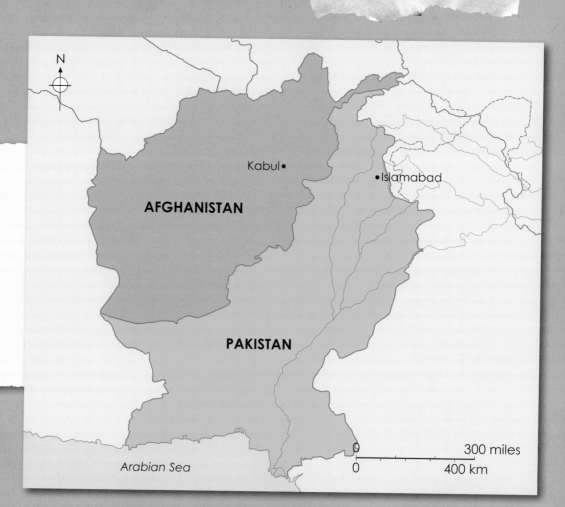

Farah and her mother joined the world's largest group of refugees when they fled from Afghanistan to Pakistan.

DAILY LIFE

In the refugee camp, Farah missed the community she knew at home. Many families lived in walled compounds in Kabul. Children played in the alleys and courtyards. Everyone knew everyone else. Children seldom went further than the school or the **bazaar** (market) a few streets away.

17

Refugees in Pakistan

In the refugee camp, Farah and her mother struggled to survive. There was never enough food or water, and there was no school for Farah to attend. Most of the time Farah's mother was too sick to work. Farah earned a little money by sewing clothes.

These Afghan refugees are receiving bags of rice and sugar in a refugee camp in Pakistan.

Hope for a new life

When Farah was 14 years old, she heard of an organization called World Relief. It helped refugees to move to the United States to start a new life. Farah and her mother applied for help. They waited in long lines and had many interviews. At last they were chosen to take the long journey across the world.

This Afghan refugee is cooking corn to sell in a refugee camp in Pakistan.

HELPING HAND

Many **non-governmental organizations (NGOs)** help refugees **emigrate** to countries where they can start new lives. Some NGOs are funded by religious groups. Others are private organizations created by people who want to help others.

Strangers in America

Farah and her mother took the long plane flight to Chicago, Illinois, in the United States. They were very frightened of the strange new country. No one spoke their language.

They lived in an apartment and did not know any of their neighbors. Instead of shopping in a friendly bazaar, they had to shop in a huge supermarket. They did not know how to cook the strange new foods and did not like the way they tasted.

Settling in

Farah started school and began to learn English. By now she was 15. She had not been to school since she was seven years old. A volunteer from a group that helped refugees became her friend. Her new friend taught her how to cope with life in the United States.

Now Farah plans to go to college. She would like to study computer science or business. She hopes to return to Afghanistan and help the people there.

These three young Afghan refugee women are posing for a photo at a college in the United States.

NUMBER CRUNCHING

In 2009 about 1.7 million Afghan refugees were living in Pakistan. Nearly one million Afghans also lived in Iran.

Iraq, 2004

Athraa Naiel Yalda lived with her family in Baghdad, the capital city of Iraq. Most people in Iraq were Muslims, but many Christians lived there, too. Athraa belonged to a Christian family.

In 2003 the United States invaded Iraq and overthrew the dictator, Saddam Hussein. The invasion began a long war and **occupation**.

These people are looking over the rubble of a Baghdad neighborhood after a bomb explosion.

Many dangers

Many Muslims hated the occupation. They thought Iraqi Christians were helping the Americans in the war. They became angry and began to attack Christian families. Thousands of Christians were forced to flee their homes.

Athraa's family hired a driver to take them across the border into Syria. Athraa and her sisters wore headscarves to disguise themselves as Muslim girls. They also had to avoid U.S. soldiers. The Americans sometimes fired on Iraqi civilians by mistake, thinking they were enemies.

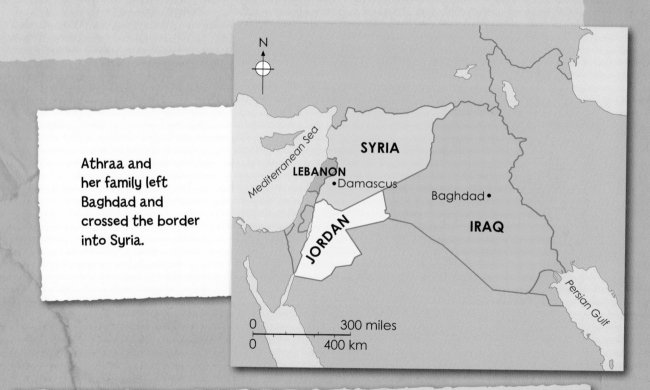

Athraa and her family left Baghdad and crossed the border into Syria.

NUMBER CRUNCHING

By 2009 nearly two million Iraqi refugees had poured into neighboring countries, especially Syria, Lebanon, and Jordan. After Afghans, Iraqis are the largest group of refugees in the world.

Outsiders in a new land

Athraa's family moved into a tiny apartment in Damascus, Syria. Many Syrians were unfriendly to the Iraqi refugees who flooded into their country. They did not welcome the new arrivals.

Some Syrian students thought that Iraqis were not as smart as Syrians. Athraa made up her mind to do her best in school and show the Syrians what Iraqis could accomplish. She studied hard and was at the top of her class.

These two Iraqi refugee children are doing homework in their apartment in a poor area of Amman, Jordan.

Plans for the future

In 2009 Athraa won a **scholarship** from an organization called United World Colleges (UWC). With help from UWC she went to Atlantic College, a school in South Wales, in the United Kingdom.

Athraa plans to study medicine. One day she wants to go back to Baghdad to work as a doctor. She would like to use her knowledge of medicine to help the police solve war crimes.

Athraa is happy that she can look forward to the future.

HELPING HAND

The Iraqi Student Project helps Iraqi students by giving them scholarships to study in the United States. It helps refugees as well as students still living in Iraq.

The Road Ahead

Many world leaders are trying to bring about peace in the Middle East. Even while the fighting continues, people in Iraq, Afghanistan, Pakistan, Israel, and Palestine are searching for solutions to their nations' problems. The road ahead will be difficult.

This refugee boy is speaking to his classmates about the Israeli attack on Lebanon in 2006.

Today and tomorrow

In books and articles, movies and news stories, refugees are beginning to tell their stories to others. As the world learns of the problems they face, more people are eager to help. They donate money to organizations that help the refugees of war build new homes and new lives, receive medical treatment and education, and plan for their future.

These Palestinian children are playing marbles in an alley in Nar Al-Bared Refugee Camp in northern Lebanon.

As refugee children grow up, they try to find a footing in new lands. They remember their painful past and seek to create a better future. Often they use the word *inshallah* ("God willing") from the **Arabic** language.

Mapping Migration

The children in this book had to become refugees. There may have been a war in their homeland. It may have been unsafe for them to stay in their own country.

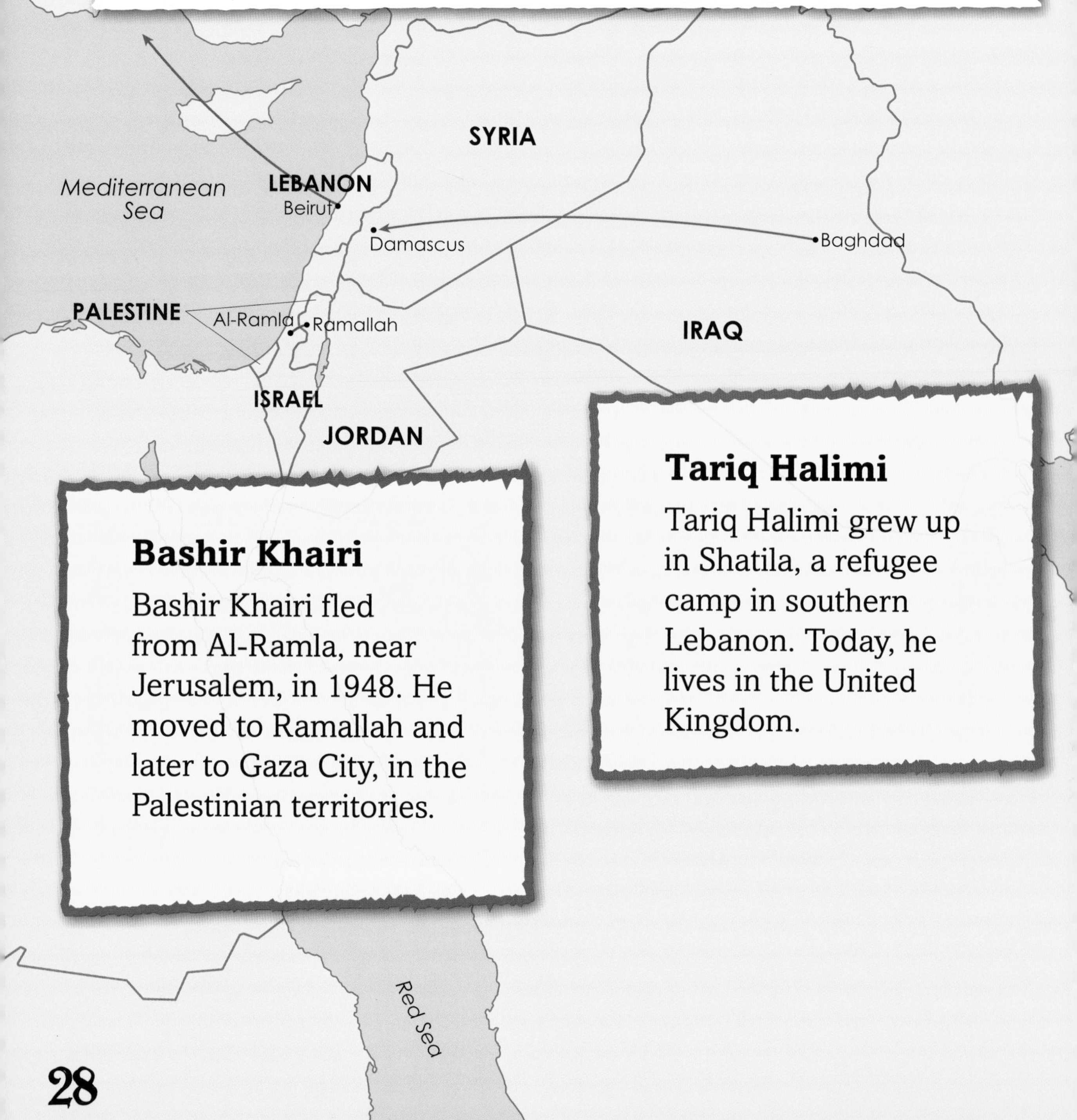

SYRIA

Mediterranean Sea

LEBANON
Beirut

Damascus

Baghdad

PALESTINE
Al-Ramla Ramallah

IRAQ

ISRAEL
JORDAN

Red Sea

Bashir Khairi

Bashir Khairi fled from Al-Ramla, near Jerusalem, in 1948. He moved to Ramallah and later to Gaza City, in the Palestinian territories.

Tariq Halimi

Tariq Halimi grew up in Shatila, a refugee camp in southern Lebanon. Today, he lives in the United Kingdom.

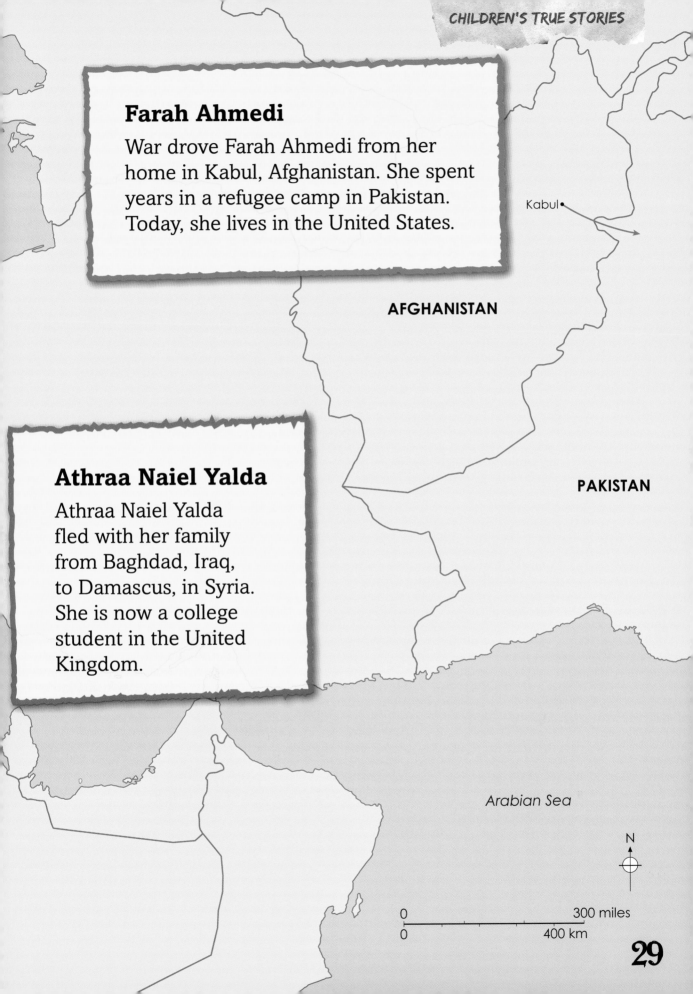

Farah Ahmedi

War drove Farah Ahmedi from her home in Kabul, Afghanistan. She spent years in a refugee camp in Pakistan. Today, she lives in the United States.

Kabul•

AFGHANISTAN

PAKISTAN

Athraa Naiel Yalda

Athraa Naiel Yalda fled with her family from Baghdad, Iraq, to Damascus, in Syria. She is now a college student in the United Kingdom.

Arabian Sea

N

| 0 | 300 miles |
| 0 | 400 km |

Glossary

Arabic language spoken widely in the Middle East

artificial not real

bazaar outdoor market, usually in an Arab country

Christianity religion based on the teachings of Jesus Christ

civilian person who does not belong to the armed forces

dictator ruler who has full control and does not allow disagreement

emigrate leave one's homeland and settle elsewhere as part of a large movement of people

Fatah Palestinian political party dedicated to the liberation of Palestine by both violent and peaceful means

Islam religion based on the teachings of the prophet Muhammad

Judaism religion of the Jewish people, based on the teachings of Moses and other prophets

landmine explosive device hidden underground. When stepped upon, it will explode.

Muslim follower of the religion of Islam. Many countries in Asia and North Africa are Muslim countries. There are groups of Muslim people living in many countries in Europe and in North America.

non-governmental organization (NGO) aid organization that is not funded or controlled by the government

occupation when the armed forces of a country invade and rule another country

rebel person who takes a stand against a government

refugee person forced to leave home to find safety outside his or her country, usually because of war or a natural disaster

scholarship gift of money to help pay for education

Taliban political group that controlled Afghanistan from 1996 to 2001

United Nations (UN) organization through which countries try to find peaceful solutions to world problems

volunteer person who works by choice without pay

World War II war that took place between 1939 and 1945. In Europe the United Kingdom, Soviet Union, United States, and their allies fought against Germany and Italy. An estimated six million Jewish people were killed in Nazi concentration camps.

Find Out More

Books

Laird, Elizabeth. *A Little Piece of Ground*. Chicago: Haymarket, 2006. This book is about a Palestinian boy living in war-torn Ramallah.

Marx, Trish, and Cindy Karp. *Sharing Our Homeland: Palestinian and Jewish Children at Summer Peace Camp*. New York: Lee & Low, 2010.

Ponsford, Simon. *Iraq* (Countries in the News). Mankato, Minn.: Smart Apple Media, 2008.

Wilson, Ruth. *Immigration* (Talking Points). Mankato, Minn.: Stargazer, 2008.

Websites

us.oneworld.net/places/middle-east
The OneWorld website provides information about refugees throughout the world, illustrated with photographs. This particular web page has up-to-date news about the Middle East.

www.learningtogive.org/lessons/unit189/lesson4.html
This is a lesson plan about the refugee experience, including a video showing interviews with five refugee children.

Museums, organizations, and other information

Arab American National Museum
13624 Michigan Avenue
Dearborn, Michigan 48126
Tel: (313) 582-2266
This museum explores Arab-American culture.

RESPECT International
www.respectrefugees.org
This organization sponsors schools for refugee children, publishes an e-zine, and runs a letter exchange between refugee and non-refugee children.

United Nations Convention on the Rights of the Child
www.unicef.org/rightsite/files/uncrcchilldfriendlylanguage.pdf
Download this document to read about the rights of all children. (Note the extra *l* in "chilldfriendly.")

Refugees International
www.refugeesinternational.org
This organization works to protect refugees and promote their rights.

Index